Broken Mirrors

Part of the 100 Poems Collection

ANGELINA SCRIPTOR

Scriptor's Ink

ISBN (Paperback): 979-8-9871239-8-0
ISBN (B&N Paperback): 978-1-971143-04-0
ISBN (Wide Distribution Paperback): 978-1-971143-17-0
ISBN (B&N Hardcover): 978-1-971143-20-0

Available in e-book and audio

Cover design by S.G. Bacon

For all of you
who focus on the cracks

And for my brother
Thank you for always being such
an enthusiastic supporter of my work
and one of my best friends
I love you

Author's Note

This poetry book is a part of Angelina Scriptor's *100 Poems Collection.*

Roses and Thorns: 100 Poems for Life, the poetry book I wrote throughout my childhood, adolescent, and teenage years, consists of exactly what the title tells: one hundred tales of life's persistent ups and downs, beauty and pain, told through the lens of poetry and the eyes of my younger self. As the years passed and I slowly entered adulthood, poetry continued to unceasingly course through me.

Inspired by the idea of my first publication, I decided to turn my poetry not only into another book, but into a collection of books. Each is filled with 100 poems, showcasing some real aspect of life, whether it be love, loss, growth, change, the passage of time, trials, or a fitting mixture of all of these and more. I plan to continue this collection throughout my own years of growth, and my hope is that my stories will shift and change with me, leaving a trail of poetry behind.

Whichever part of this collection you have stumbled upon, for whatever reason you may be reading, I desire for you to know that you're reading a part of me, whether it be my own experiences, those I've witnessed, or the ones brought upon by my innermost thoughts, feelings, and emotions. Perhaps you'll see those around you, or maybe even a part of yourself. I hope you enjoy my work, but even more so, I pray you will find whatever it might be that you're looking for.

Please feel encouraged to read my work in any order you desire, as well as the poems themselves. Find what calls to you, and listen.

With hope and blessings,
Angelina

I never asked to be a poet
but the words overflowed my head
so when I turned to poetry
I guess it just made sense

So I asked to write a poem
and I was overflowed with pain
But if poems are my song
then I was given these times to sing

We were born with wings
wings to explore—inspire—soar
But those wings were made of glass
and shattered
before we were fully born

She makes it a goal
to try to be seen
She smiles at strangers
but what does that mean?

All she is craving
is one simple touch
For is smiling back
really so much
to ask?

I light a dozen candles
just to plagiarize their tune
Their melodies
of whispered flames
beg my heart to see them through

She said 'I don't do that'
She said 'not who I am'
Now, all these years later,
She's the only one who understands

Take me to a garden
as you whisper in my ear

Then throw me in the ivy
because I shed a tear

I had a dream about your lover
but I swear it's not like that
Because your lover was a monster
who haunts my dreams and back

Can you imagine a place
where everyone you see
is gold

We would fall for each other
before we even got the chance
to grow old

She met a boy
with beautiful eyes—
and those eyes she can't forget

They stayed with her
embroidered in her brain—
after she found him dead

I still await your call
a call within the dark
a call so full of anger
it will scare away the night

When she bites her tongue
until it bleeds
why be surprised
as it comes off clean?

A word comes bitter
silence oft' speaks
tired commitment
dulls the rosiest of cheeks

We go about each day
living on repeat
keeping in our step
thinking how we breathe

Imagine if we smiled
if each day was remembered
as a new chance
a new beginning
a new start

Imagine if we took that chance
to live

Hold a sigh
repress a laugh
for poetry
stems from the black

It brings her pain
but the pain is relief
To lay off her heart
until she can breathe

It's tight in her chest
while her mind is much worse
If she doesn't exhale
she is sure she will burst

There's a drawbridge by
the Castle doors
Made of strong but
rotting wood

The princess lies
somewhere inside
Her knight won't free her
though he could

She tells him then
to run and hide
Don't let his armor rust
for her

'Til the drawbridge falls
he'll heed her calls
Both waiting on
the other

He’s a wolf among flowers
looking for sheep to devour
But he’ll never realize
they’re all weeds in disguise
Always pulling him in
and wearing him thin

The car is on fire
there's flames all around
You hold onto her face
and say you don't hear a sound

They say that heroes never die
that their names go on and on
But at this point I'm wondering
if their stories are all wrong

You picked apart every word
as if you were designed
as the ultimate critic

I sat, and I stared, listened close
with a nod. Didn't bother
to tell you
who wrote it

A bleeding heart
is much too young
to bleed out dry
under the sun

Before it rots
it burns with pain
but hurts much more
when long the same

Momma can't stop crying
and Daddy's really mad
Sister's in denial
and Brother says she's bad

it was just a little note
one not meant to be seen
but ever since they found it
she's been living life in pleas

I know your darkest secrets
but I can't say that I do
For you said you'd wished to tell me
but you're not ready to

Sunlight shifting
Start to think
Keep your focus
Never blink

Time moves slowly
If you wait
But don't get lost
In passing days

She can never sleep
Then again, what's new?
Talking to herself
until the afternoon

'Can anybody save me?'
she'll whisper really close
then she'll realize
that no one's ever home

Sometimes there's only
So much you can do
When they're dying to fall
You must let them fall through

And while it's hard to let go
Perhaps not for the best
It was their wish
Even when led them to death

If a prayer
is enough
to from your lowest
lift you up

Why do we never
stop to plead
and instead drown
in human greed?

She's embarrassed to be nude in front of her
parents
Even though, they raised her, with love
For she knows, if she strips down, they'll see
her
and how hurt covers her like a robe

There was a painting with my name
you would hang upon your wall
There was a painting with my name
you'd never pick up when it'd fall

If he's a prince
then she's the queen
If he likes letters
he'd spell her
"perfectly"

Whatever he does
she does it best
But he remembers
the first hairs on her head

I was too tired
and you hadn't slept
our hearts were on fire
and our souls needed rest

It wasn't our fault
when the lines got too blurred
for far in the night
is when feelings ought stir

You never know who has a camera
so in everything you do
act as if someone is watching
Lest you'll say "I never knew"

They sealed her mouth tight shut
begging her not to sing
But when they heard her hum
they undid the stitch with glee

Call then not for silence
or the easiest answer
For you might be missing out
on the inside's hidden worth

"It's getting bad again," she said
So he took her to the castle where they met
Climbed the highest tower
while she leaned over the edge
She took in a deep breath
and then over it he sent her
Down
Until she was underground

They asked him why she jumped that day
While tearing up he'd always say
It was too much pain to stay
So fly

Air
is one of the
most

Tantalizing forms of
raging
untapped
existence

If you're someone's lover
why did you come near?
If you're someone's lover
why give her that fear?

He wriggles out of bed
as if he was a worm
May as well
because right now
he surrounds himself with dirt

It was not softness
she was feeling
but bitter
to hollow
to empty
which simply felt nicer
than the feelings
from before

Every scar is a story
whether great or lame or small

so be wary where you cut
lest you bleed and must tell all

Quid sum faciens
Getting locked in a dark room
Nemo, nothing, nihil
My heart playing out of tune

Auxilium petens
I think I lost the key
Expecto, expectare
You said that you would save me

She drank too much water
while pretending it was wine
Either way, she's in her room
losing her insides

Imagine every moment
Imagine every bright star
was left here just for you
to make living less sub-par

Imagine every smallest twinkle
too many there to count
was painted just to make you smile
For if not that, then why else?

She always knew that she would make it
she always knew that she'd survive
at some point it just was buried
in pain of feeling the need to hide

She adopted becoming an outcast
when she knew that's not who she was
for at least a label was something
to lead her onwards into the light

If Icarus hadn't had fallen
but escaped
to fly so free

Would we still remember his tale?
or was it simply
meant to be?

Through the night I lie awake
although I've got nothing to do
My brain, it keeps on ticking
and my heart, it is the fuse

I passed an old car
that smelled
like nail polish

And I don't know
what that means

But the gray couple
with the top down
seemed as happy
as can be

Promise that you love me
say you won't let go
Because I'm about to jump
and need someone to keep me whole

I once knew a girl
with a broken head
She would pop a pill
just to make her bed
Then she'd take another
to cover all the dread
Always did it over
'gain and again
While her sister prayed
to never find her dead

Don’t write down every letter
but don't let yourself forget
Don’t exist through memories
but don’t live with that regret

With every king
comes great tragedy
or greater travesty

Why must the artist starve
to overflow with inspiration

And then why must the poet bleed
for her words to be considered?

Call it not 'insecurity'
or a broken tongue
But instead
look to the things
that have made them numb

There's a train's call in the distance
and I wonder where it went
for the tracks were torn down years ago
and they filled the space in with cement

What is a message
if there's no one to hear
or if there are many
but you speak less than clear?

Do you keep your thoughts sewn
tied tight with a knot
or do you let them all flow
and leave hearts falling distraught?

I wish I could capture this moment
when life is still, yet dark
as night

They say a picture's worth a thousand words
but, alas, blinded
I write

For every page
that she can flip
is one less drink
she craves to sip

When she tried to look up to her Moon
a tree was blocking her view
She climbed it to get back to you

Then the final branch broke from its mound
She plummeted all the way down
but smiled as she hit the ground

I fought so hard to beat the dragon
to keep a blade far from my skin
But as soon as I saw your eyes
I knew I'd let you in

My words escaped in one breath
a secret—never tell
I don't want to be a knight
but a princess kissed farewell

Would a songbird sing
past noon
If canaries flew in
and stole
her tune?

I try to imagine
every star in the sky
as a forgotten whisper
as a dream long bled dry

They glow in the dark
too many to count
as they speak to your heart
while you can't hear their sound

It's perpetual sadness
that's been haunting her brain
She don't know where she's going
but she don't want to stay

Walking 'round in circles
while trying to pray
But always, on the inside
she's barely awake

To make a pact
is to hold the knife
and whatever drips
are the words ahead

If she is a better poet than I
what is the point to all my words?
Does she do it for the fame or
does she do it to stop the hurt?

They called him Atlas
without seeing his back
They named her Persephone
without kissing the black

Stole out his weight
before seeing him bleed
Took her away
without seeing her need

Is it a burden
if it's all he knew
And can it be love
if it's what she holds true

Inspiration
is a weary tale
when it strikes you
late at night

Vision blurried
heart untied
it whispers of
soft might

They say it happens to every woman
but still I'm left untouched
They call me pure
but insecure
is how I'd name my head

So I wait until the moment
where I finally become one of them
They call it wrong
but I sing this song
because they're filled with dread

Death is not illegal
Nor is it always not a choice
And on that some linger too long
As to never lose their voice

Not every death has forlorn meaning
Nor is every memory not forgot
But in some infrequent moments
Infamous choices take their lot

His father isn't kind
but his mother, she is blind
so again she asks her son
to fetch the trash

He hurries down the hill
always careful not to spill
but somewhere along the way
he dropped a match

Now once he's back inside
being perfectly polite
he's met with certain lashes
to his back

He took it all with pride
recognizing father's wine
for what's an empty bottle
compared to that?

If the picture's watered down
how could you see that she had drowned?

It seemed so far away to you
yet she'd always said her heart was bruised

Apollo's golden chariot
could only carry so much weight
For after Icarus fell
not even Sun could feel the same

She said she hated poetry
then she'd bleed until she sung

She said she hated church
then fell in love with the pastor's son

Do you remember that time
it was you, your mother, and I
as we three sat down to dine?

She asked me not to be a stranger
I smiled, waved "See you later"
you expressed an evening divine

But I never saw her again
No, nor I you, my friend
yet I believe we shan't make amends

If only I had watched the time
for, as they say, it flies
especially when secrets are nigh

There were dried
tears on her face
when she met your eyes
said "I'm okay"

And when you stood
straight up and left
you taught her what
those two words meant

The wildflower grows
despite who showers her
Reaches out for the sun
by her own means

When Man comes along
and plucks her from her growing place
Left to wilt
and wither
forgotten
on her own

Perhaps her message
will spread
with her seed

I was never the snooping type
until after what you did
Tore out my heart, picked it apart
and then pinned it back in

A boy hates his mother
although she raised him well

And a man hates his castle
until the day it fell

Imagination
cannot hurt you
‘less there’s nothing else
to do

For the most
dangerous time’s
when you’ve got nothing left
to lose

Button eyes
stare from the shelf
down to the bed
that brings her hell

Can someone save her
from herself
she's getting lonely
with all farewells

Golden pen
Silver sword
Mighty moon
David's chord

While one is alright
with losing his head
is the other okay
just observing that dread?

They continue with life
as a repeated cause
never breaking the cycle
or ever viewing what was

I dreamed a dream
I bled myself through
all over your new carpet and shoes

I let you lead
I jumped from your roof
but I'd stolen your own parachute

Time passes slowly
to the one who waits
But restless hearts
beat on and on
and do not stop
for days

Goodbye
to the ones
that brought
him here

Goodbye
to the place
always filling
with fear

Goodbye
everything
you won't
be missed

Goodbye
dreaded head
once sealed
with a kiss

Listen
on the mountain tops
where the birds
find their homes

The air there
seems much clearer
as you try to take it
down the road

The peacefulness
escapes you
as it slips through
broken fingers

You must keep it
still unseen
for deep within you
none can reach it

She'd go to bed, at four a.m.
even when she'd need wake up at five

close her eyes, pray something unholy
close her eyes, she'd pray to die

She'd sleep the day, beg it would fade
even when it was all in her head

For when you sleep, at four a.m.
harmonies are dissonance

I imagine this small pen as a blade
as I carve the meanings of my words
deep in the soul of my page

You tell me that I'm pretty
you think that I'm so smart
Tell me that there's nothing
when compared to my heart

But you haven't seen my scars
you haven't been inside
You haven't faced my demons
when I've nothing left to hide

Suspicious stains along the carpet
a sewing needle by the door
Ask her what she did past curfew
she'll say it's nothing I haven't before

Run
Run faster
you can't escape
your mind

Overdrive
kicks in
you've left them all
behind

But they never did
you made it up
and the silence now
sinks in

You're running from
a memory
rather than
what is

They say blood is thicker than water
so be careful where you tread

I can't remember the last time
I wanted to see you again

For if blood is thicker than water
you mustn't jump right in

If she sang a darker tune
would you still hold her so close?
If he spoke his memories
would you bid him now to go?

Every lost soul has a secret
that they're careful not to show
but stay with them as it passes
and without words you then will know

We ask to find the proof
to know that You are there
but the honest truth
is that You are everywhere

You're in the gentlest of breeze
that sways the sunlit trees
You're in the changing of the skies
rotating with the seasons

You're in the raging of a storm
that turns out all our lights
and the most beautiful of stars
to get us through our darkest nights

Lord, You're all around us
in Your beauty do You show
You're in the smallest of our whispers
just waiting for us to know

Starve the artist
Steal the crown
Burn the witches
Slow things down

Lock the maiden
Trap her in
In all you do
You let them win

Sunsets
Pink skies
Gray clouds
Blue eyes

Come in
Think twice
Spiked drink
Sharp knife

Wrap me in blankets
Free from my song
Drown out my tune
Pretend not all is wrong

Fill me with silence
Ignore every plea
Force my page to turn
And on I may keep

A dragon braced the bridge
Where a sword was left akin
Both there to guard their place
Sullen, lost, and braced

One fierce and mighty stewed
While the other cold, construed
Abandoned by his master
After attacking the fiery dancer

The knight had thought he'd bring his peace
While the dragon then would sleep
Now can never bow her head
After stopping Sir Knight in dread

Why are you so angry
that the sun rose again?
Why be filled with suffering
when beauty does here stick?

Each day is a lesson
no less than a gift
So don't drink it like poison
instead allow your soul to lift

No one knows the difference
if you pave the Castle in your mind
And no one knows the difference
if you leave the pain behind

If you knew you died
after hours
would you still stay up
past ten?

If you knew you died
picking flowers
would you still stop to smell
their scent?

Are you living life
knowing it will end
or do you spend your nights
whispering regrets?

Truly I am a poet
although I never meant to be
For as I write my verses
my heart sings out of key

I used to watch the raindrops
as they raced along the glass
Until my focus shifted
and I only saw its cracks

For a long time I was sad
once I'd noticed how it shattered
Then my vision cleared again
for the reflection was what mattered

Acknowledgements

"God, if You are willing to help me finish this poetry book, I'd love to use it to honor You in some way."

Those were the words I thought while on what I call an "inspiration walk," attempting to clear my head, pray, and gain ideas for whatever would come to mind.

The next day, I reviewed my notebook to transfer my freshly-thought-of poems to my work-in-progress poetry books, the first of which I had planned and been eager to publish for three years.

I found that, during my walk, I had written the exact number of poems I needed, with exactly the right themes, to finish *Broken Mirrors*.

There is such an active and present God looking out for and watching over us, working in our daily lives. One all-powerful and all-knowing, yet still so loving that He would send His only begotten Son to die the most painful, humiliating death on a cross to take our place. In doing so, He paid the price for the endless sins that we all commit, and, by raising Him again, He is offering us the opportunity to be forgiven, saved, and spend eternity in joy by His side, if only we put our faith in Him, repent, and believe in Jesus' sacrifice. If you haven't yet personally met this God, call out to Him. Jesus died for you, no matter who you are or what you've been through, no matter how lost or how broken you may feel, or even if you've thought you were better off without Him. The Creator of our universe is waiting for you with a Father's love. He *wants* to hear from you, and He's ready to call you His own.

Thank you to my family and friends who supported and encouraged me as I committed to the writing, editing, formatting, and publication of this book, finally beginning this long-awaited collection. It has been a journey to get here, and much has changed since I first began writing, but I hope the years that have passed will make for an even greater story.

Thank you, dear reader, for spending this time in my collection. I hope you were able to gain something from it, to see something you may not have before, or to at least recognize that someone else has spent these feelings with you.

You are not alone. Your Heavenly Father and I love you.

Until my next book,
Angelina Scriptor

Also By Angelina Scriptor

Roses and Thorns:
100 Poems for Life

Trees of Fate

About the Author

Angelina Scriptor

After graduating high school with highest honors and the state-certified Seal of Biliteracy in Latin and English, Angelina Scriptor instantly began to pursue her lifelong dream of becoming an author. Since then, she has (accidentally) embarked on a poetry journey, publishing *Roses and Thorns: 100 Poems for Life* at the age of 18, and now working on her *100 Poems Collection,* a project she hopes to add to throughout her lifetime. She is also known for her debut novel, *Trees of Fate*, and is eager to continue the fiction writing that has always stolen her heart, including a medieval fantasy novel series that she hopes to publish throughout her twenties... all while being distracted by whatever idea interrupts her train of thought next.

She can also be found on Instagram
(@Angelina.Scriptor)

www.ingramcontent.com/pod-product-compliance
Lightning Source LLC
LaVergne TN
LVHW051012080826
845145LV00009B/2582

* 9 7 8 1 9 7 1 1 4 3 1 7 0 *